BE YOUR OWN BOSS

PLAN A CAR WASH

STEPHANE HILLARD

PowerKiDS press
New York

Published in 2021 by The Rosen Publishing Group, Inc.
29 East 21st Street, New York, NY 10010

Copyright © 2021 by The Rosen Publishing Group, Inc.

All rights reserved. No part of this book may be reproduced in any form without permission in writing from the publisher, except by a reviewer.

First Edition

Portions of this work were originally authored by Emma Carlson Berne and published as *Run Your Own Car Wash*. All new material in this edition authored by Stephane Hillard.

Editor: Elizabeth Krajnik
Book Design: Reann Nye

Photo Credits: Cover Oli_Trolly/iStock/Getty Images Plus/Getty Images; series art stas11/Shutterstock.com; p. 5 Jerritt Clark/Getty Images Entertainment/Getty Images; p. 7 Anna Kraynova/Shutterstock.com; p. 9 Cavan Images/Cavan/Getty Images; pp. 11, 15 Peopleimages/E+/Getty Images; p. 13 Jupiterimages/Creatas/Getty Images Plus/Getty Images; p. 17 firina/iStock/Getty Images Plus/Getty Imges; p. 19 Ronnachai Palas/Shutterstock.com; p. 21 moodboard/moodboard/Getty Images Plus/Getty Images; p. 22 gchutka/E+/Getty Images.

Library of Congress Cataloging-in-Publication Data

Names: Hillard, Stephane, author.
Title: Plan a car wash / Stephane Hillard.
Description: New York : PowerKids Press, [2021] | Series: Be your own boss | Includes index.
Identifiers: LCCN 2020001339 | ISBN 9781725318977 (paperback) | ISBN 9781725318991 (library binding) | ISBN 9781725318984 (6 pack)
Subjects: LCSH: Car washes-Juvenile literature. | Car wash industry-Juvenile literature. | Money-making projects for children-Juvenile literature.
Classification: LCC HD9999.C272 H55 2021 | DDC 629.2/60288-dc23
LC record available at https://lccn.loc.gov/2020001339

Manufactured in the United States of America

Some of the images in this book illustrate individuals who are models. The depictions do not imply actual situations or events.

CPSIA Compliance Information: Batch #CSPK20. For Further Information contact Rosen Publishing, New York, New York at 1-800-237-9932.

CONTENTS

BECOMING AN ENTREPRENEUR 4
SUPPLY AND DEMAND 6
CREATING A BUSINESS PLAN 8
EXPENSES AND BUDGETING..........10
THE IMPORTANCE OF ADVERTISING...................12
PLAN CAREFULLY 14
GATHERING SUPPLIES..................16
CAR WASH DAY! 18
A JOB FOR EVERYONE 20
BUSINESS CHECKLIST 22
GLOSSARY.............................23
INDEX................................24
WEBSITES 24

BECOMING AN ENTREPRENEUR

Do you often ask your parents for money to go out with your friends? Or maybe you're trying to save money for college or to travel later in life. If you'd like to make money and be your own boss, then you might be a budding entrepreneur. An entrepreneur is a person who starts a business and is willing to possibly lose money in order to make money.

This book will show you the steps to follow to plan and start your own business, including making a business plan, creating a **budget**, advertising, and more. In time, you'll be able to enjoy your business's **profits**.

Kids can be entrepreneurs too! When Moziah Bridges was just nine years old, he came up with the idea for Mo's Bows, a company that makes and sells handmade bow ties.

5

SUPPLY AND DEMAND

The purpose of a business is to provide a product or service for people. Your business should fulfill a need or a want in your community. Make a list of products or services you think you could provide. Then do some **research**. You can avoid **competition** by offering a product or service that isn't already being provided.

Running car washes could be a great business for you. All cars get dirty, and when they do, their owners will look around for a car wash. To make the most money, follow the steps on the next few pages.

GOOD BUSINESS
In some places, there aren't many car washes. This means that you're sure to make a good chunk of change—especially if you're quick and have good prices.

Ask your parents if it's OK to practice washing the family car. You can also ask your neighbors if you can wash their car. You might choose to do it for free or at a lower price because you're still learning. This will help you wash cars faster and do a better job.

CREATING A BUSINESS PLAN

Before you have your car wash, you'll need to create a business plan. This plan outlines where, when, and how you'll run your business. First, where will you hold your car wash? Pick a spot with faucets nearby for your **hoses**. Think about how much space there is for cars to get in and out and wait in line.

Next, decide when you want to hold your car wash. You should choose a time when most people aren't at work, such as a weekend.

How will you run your car wash business? Will you hire help? Think of the supplies you'll need for advertising and the car wash.

GOOD BUSINESS

If you decide to hold your car wash in a space you don't own, such as a parking lot, you'll need to get **permission** from the person in charge of that place and ask whether there's a fee to use the space.

Before your car wash, you need to give yourself enough time to plan, shop for supplies, make your advertising signs and flyers, and hire helpers.

EXPENSES AND BUDGETING

Your car wash business, like all other businesses, will have expenses. Expenses are costs that arise throughout the course of doing business. Creating a budget for your car wash business will allow you to keep track of your expenses. Your expenses will help you figure out how much you should charge your customers.

After you've created your budget, check how much money you have saved. Do you have enough saved to run your business for the first month? If not, you'll need to borrow some money, most likely from your parents. Then you'll need to make a plan to repay them.

GOOD BUSINESS

When creating your budget, your expenses should include all the supplies you'll need to buy. You can save money by using supplies you already own or shopping around to find the best price for your supplies.

How many car washes do you think you'll need to do to replace the savings you used to start your business and to cover all your other expenses? Does that number work for you? If not, you may need to increase the price of each car wash.

THE IMPORTANCE OF ADVERTISING

Advertising is how you'll let people know you're planning to hold a car wash. You can advertise by telling people, which is called word of mouth, by making a flashy flyer or sign, or by putting an ad in your local newspaper. Be sure to include the date, time, and location of your car wash on your advertising signs and flyers.

Making signs to post around town and flyers to drop in people's mailboxes or hand out at school will keep your advertising expenses low. However, you need to get permission from your school or city officials before posting your signs. There may be rules about who can post and where.

GOOD BUSINESS
You can include other information on your signs, such as any **discounts** or specials you might be offering or if any of the profits will be **donated** to **charity**. This may bring in more business.

To make your signs and flyers you'll need poster board, markers, paint, tape, and other supplies. Don't forget to put the cost of these supplies in your budget!

PLAN CAREFULLY

Running a car wash business takes a lot of planning. Car washes take up a lot of room and require special supplies, such as hoses, water, and places for cars to park. You'll have to think carefully about where you want to hold your car wash. You should also think about the time of day. If it's around or after noon, it may be too hot depending on where you live.

You might want to hire people to help you run your car wash business. Ask your friends if they want to be **employees**. You can pay them a flat fee or you can pay them by the hour. Remember to include your employees' wages in your budget.

Having a friend help you with your car wash may make the time pass by quicker. You may even have a fun time washing cars with them!

GATHERING SUPPLIES

A few days before your car wash, you should gather the supplies you already have and put them in one spot. Then, ask a parent to bring you to a store where you can buy the supplies you still need, such as buckets and large sponges.

Save all the **receipts** for the items you've purchased. When you get home, put the supplies you purchased with the supplies you already have. After you've held your car wash, subtract the cost of the supplies you purchased from the money you made. If you made more money than you spent on your supplies, you made a profit.

GOOD BUSINESS

Be sure to keep track of who lent you supplies. You can write this down in a notebook to make it easier when it's time to return the supplies.

You may be able to borrow some supplies from other family members, neighbors, or friends. This will help you keep your expenses low.

CAR WASH DAY!

Now that you've created your business plan, made a budget, advertised, and gathered your supplies, you're ready for business! If you're holding your car wash at a parking lot, load the car for the ride to the wash site. If you're holding your car wash at home, get your supplies ready to go. Hang a large, flashy sign so people know where to park their car.

You'll need a waterproof box to collect money. Make sure you have small bills to make change. Write down how many cars you wash and how much each person paid. This will help you later when you're counting your money.

If the weather on the day of your car wash is warm and sunny, that can make it even more enjoyable!

A JOB FOR EVERYONE

If you've hired employees, each of them should have a job. One person can welcome new cars, another can collect money, someone else can be in charge of soaping the car, and another person can rinse and dry the car. If you've decided to do the car wash without help, you'll do all these jobs yourself.

At the end of the car wash, pay your employees and clean up. Return any supplies you borrowed. Add up the money in your cash box and subtract the amount you started the day with. However much you have left is your profit!

Don't forget to subtract the cost of your supplies from the money you make during your car wash!

BUSINESS CHECKLIST

- Address a community need
- Create a business plan
- Create a budget
- Purchase car wash and advertising supplies
- Advertise your car wash
- Hire employees
- Set up your car wash
- Get down to business
- Enjoy the profits

GLOSSARY

budget: A plan used to decide the amount of money that can be spent and how it will be spent.

charity: An organization or fund for helping the needy.

competition: A person or group you're trying to succeed against.

discount: An amount taken off a regular price.

donate: To give as a way of helping people in need.

employee: A person who is paid to work for another.

hose: A long, usually rubber tube through which liquids or gases can flow.

permission: The approval of a person in authority.

profit: The gain after all the expenses are subtracted from the total amount received.

receipt: A piece of paper on which the things you buy or the services you pay for are listed with the total amount paid and the prices for each.

research: Careful study that is done to find and report new knowledge about something.

INDEX

A
advertising, 4, 9, 12, 18, 22

B
borrow, 10, 17, 20
Bridges, Moziah, 5
budget, 4, 10, 13, 14, 18, 22
business plan, 4, 8, 18, 22

C
competition, 6
customer, 10

D
discount, 12

E
employee, 14, 20, 22
entrepreneur, 4, 5
expense, 10, 11, 17

M
money, 4, 6, 10, 16, 18, 20, 21
Mo's Bows, 5

P
product, 6
profit, 4, 16, 20, 22

S
service, 6
supplies, 8, 9, 10, 11, 13, 14, 16, 17, 18, 20, 21, 22

W
wage, 14
word of mouth, 12

WEBSITES

Due to the changing nature of Internet links, PowerKids Press has developed an online list of websites related to the subject of this book. This site is updated regularly. Please use this link to access the list: www.powerkidslinks.com/byoboss/carwash